The Origin of the Dai Bamboo House

By Sunshine Orange Studio

Translated by Fang Fan

Adapted by Joe Gregory

Books Beyond Boundaries

ROYAL COLLINS

The Origin of the Dai Bamboo House

By Sunshine Orange Studio
Translated by Fang Fan
Adapted by Joe Gregory

First published in 2022 by Royal Collins Publishing Group Inc.
Groupe Publication Royal Collins Inc.
BKM Royalcollins Publishers Private Limited

Headquarters: 550-555 boul. René-Lévesque O Montréal (Québec) H2Z1B1 Canada
India office: 805 Hemkunt House, 8th Floor, Rajendra Place, New Delhi 110 008

Original Edition © Yunnan Education Publishing House Co., Ltd.

ISBN: 978-1-4878-1015-3

To find out more about our publications, please visit www.royalcollins.com.

In the old days, the Dai people did not live
in houses. They made their homes in caves.

There was a goddess who was sad when she saw her sweet Dai people suffer, so she sent a wise man named Payasangmudi to be the leader of the Dai people and help them solve this problem.

Payasangmudi was very wise! He invented many useful tools and everyday objects, like farming tools such as hoes and ploughs, as well as kitchen objects like bowls, pots, and chopsticks, and taught them how to make pottery.

Under the leadership of Payasangmudi, the population of the Dai people grew rapidly and soon the caves were no longer big enough for everyone. Payasangmudi thought to himself, "Where else could we live?"

One day, it suddenly started raining. Payasangmudi saw how the people who did not have time to run for shelter cut down big banana leaves and used them as protection from the rain.

This gave Payasangmudi an idea. He used tree trunks to make a frame and covered it with banana leaves and thatch to make a flat-roofed hut. To test it, Payasangmudi moved out of the cave to live in the hut.

However, as the rain started falling, the hut was leaking, leaving no dry places, so Payasangmudi had no choice but to move back to the cave.

Later, when Payasangmudi was out hunting, he was again caught in a heavy rain. He took shelter under a tree, with his dog sitting down beside him. With its head held high, its front legs straight, and its tail on the ground, Payasangmudi saw how the rainwater would slide down the dog's back.

He thought to himself, "If I made a sloped roof for the hut, would it be able to keep out the rain?"

Payasangmudi was sure that he had solved the problem, but when a violent storm broke out, he realized that he had failed again. The wind blew the rain into the hut, and it flooded once more.

The goddess was deeply moved when she saw how Payasangmudi
kept building houses, despite failing again and again. She decided
to help Payasangmudi. One rainy day, she turned into a beautiful
phoenix, and flew down to the world.

The phoenix landed in front of Payasangmudi, spreading her wide and beautiful wings and stood upright to form the shape of the Chinese character "介" (jiè). But Payasangmudi was still confused.

The phoenix said, "Payasangmudi, look carefully at my wings. See if they can keep out the wind and rain. Now, look at my feet. Can they support a roof that can keep out the wind and rain?"

Payasangmudi put his hands together and saluted the phoenix. He carefully observed the upright phoenix's wings, and he understood what she was trying to tell him.

Payasangmudi immediately started building a house, using the plan of the goddess.

As Payasangmudi was finishing building the frame, a strong gust of wind caused the frame to fall down. The strongest, tallest center post broke in the middle.

Payasangmudi had to go to the mountains to find a new center post. He looked everywhere, but just could not find the right one. That night, Payasangmudi laid awake, worrying about the center post.

At dawn, he heard a loud noise coming from Heaven. As he looked around, he saw a straight tree trunk right outside the cave. He had found his center post. Payasangmudi knew that the goddess had helped him, so he hurried to thank her.

Payasangmudi started cutting the tree trunk to turn it into the right size for a center post. But as he put it into the ground, it quickly started sinking. A bottomless hole appeared, swallowing the post.

It kept falling and falling until finally, it fell with a "boom" into the Dragon King's Palace at the bottom of the ocean. The Dragon King knew that the post did not belong to his palace, so he ordered his subjects to use all their strength to move out the post, and return it to Payasangmud.

Payasangmudi asked the Dragon King why the post kept sinking. The Dragon King told Payasangmudi, "This is a sinking post. It is lazy. If you, a human, use it as a center post, it will sink. If you don't want it to sink, you must use the leaves of the Dongdao and Dongmang trees as its base. The leaves of Dongdao trees have a supporting force and the leaves of Dongmang trees can hold the base firmly."

Payasangmudi went to the mountains to find the leaves of the Dongdao and the Dongmang trees. He laid the two kinds of leaves on the ground and the center post stood firm and did not sink. Payasangmudi then built a strong house frame of bamboo, with the center post in the middle.

After many failures, Payasangmudi finally built a tall bamboo house. The house had two stories; the upper one was used to protect the people from the rain and the lower one was used for their livestock. The ridges were like the phoenix's spreading wings, guiding the rain down the sides, so that people could live comfortably in the house.

After the Dai people moved into bamboo houses, they never forgot Payasangmudi, and his gift to them of bamboo houses.